Just
Continue
Buying

Tested Strategies for Saving Money
and Increasing Wealth

by

Ben O. Rowe

Table of contents

Just continue buying

Introduction

Many people aim to become wealthy, yet doing so can frequently seem like a challenging undertaking. Avoid being seduced by get-rich-quick schemes and possibilities which seem too good to be true because they could lead you down a dangerous path. Achieving this objective requires patience, perseverance, and discipline.

The good news is that anyone can build and maintain money over time by using specific ideas and tactics. Also, your odds of success are increased the earlier you begin using these.

Savings can offer a lot more advantages than just financial security. Due to rising interest rates, you could pay off high-interest debt like credit cards with more substantial savings. Financial experts advise getting out of debt as quickly as possible in light of today's unstable economical environment.

To begin with, having some money enables you to prevent incurring additional debt to pay for initial purchases. Also, you would have more freedom to experiment professionally and take more chances without having to worry as much about how your income might be damaged.

Now that we know it's necessary to save money, the next question is how much should we save?

Chapter 1

Ways to save your money

Budgeting & Saving
Having a plan makes saving simpler; use this
guide to make one.

Starting to save money can occasionally be
the most challenging part. This step-by-step
manual can assist you in creating a
straightforward and practical plan that will
enable you to save for all of your immediate
and long-term objectives:

1. Keep track of your costs.
   The first step in saving money is to
   calculate your current spending.
   Maintain a record of every penny you
   spend, including regular monthly
   payments and purchases for groceries,
   coffee, and other home items. Using a
   pen and paper, a straightforward
   spreadsheet, a free online expenditure
   tracker, or an app, record your

expenses as is most convenient for you. Once you have your data, group the figures into mortgage, petrol, and food categories and total each sum. Make sure you've included everything by consulting your bank and credit card statements.

2. Plan to save money in your budget. You can start making a budget now that you know how much money you spend each month. To organize your spending and prevent overspending, your budget should illustrate how your expenses compare to your income. Make sure to account for costs like car maintenance that happen frequently but not every month. Add a savings category in your spending plan and try to save money up to a level that feels comfortable to you at first. Eventually, aim to increase

your savings by up to 15–20% of your income.

3. Look for ways to reduce expenses. It could be time to make spending cuts if you aren't able to save as much money as you'd want. Determine the non-essentials you can do without, such as entertainment and eating out. Look for ways to cut costs on your fixed monthly bills, such as your cell phone plan and auto insurance. Additional suggestions for reducing daily spending include:

- Establishing a budget

- How to reduce your monthly expenses

- Look for free things to do.
  To find free or cheap
  entertainment, use sites like local
  event calendars.

- Examine recurring fees
  Renewing memberships and
  subscriptions should be canceled,
  mainly if you don't utilize them.
- Compare the costs of cooking at
  home with eating out.
- Prepare most of your meals at
  home, and when you want to
  reward yourself, look into local
  restaurant specials.
- Delay making a purchase.
- Wait a few days before making
  an unnecessary purchase when
  tempted. The item might be
  something you want rather than

need, so you make a strategy to save for it.

4. Plan your savings.
   Setting a goal is one of the best methods to save money. Start by considering your potential savings goals, short-term (one to three years) and long-term (four or more years). Decide how much money you'll need and how long it might take you to save it, and then make an estimate.

5. Decide what your top financial priorities are.
   Your goals will likely significantly influence how you manage your savings after spending and income. For instance, you may start saving money for a new automobile immediately if you know you'll soon need to replace

your old one. But keep in mind long-term objectives as well; it's critical that retirement planning be addressed in favor of pressing immediate concerns. You can clearly understand how to allocate your savings if you know how to prioritize your saving objectives.

6. Choose the appropriate equipment. Several savings and investment accounts are appropriate for short- and long-term objectives. And you're not required to select just one. Choose the combination that will help you save money for your goals most effectively by carefully examining all the possibilities and considering balance minimums, fees, interest rates, risk, and when you'll need the money.

- Short-term objectives
  Choose one of these FDIC-insured bank accounts if you'll need the money soon or require quick access to it:

- An escrow account
  A certificate of deposit (CD) secures your funds for a predetermined amount of time at a rate often more significant than a savings account.

- Long-term objectives
  Think about the following whether you're investing for retirement or your child's education:

- Equities like stocks, mutual funds, and individual retirement accounts (IRAs) or 529 plans are tax-advantaged savings accounts. Through investing accounts with a broker-dealer1, these investment products are accessible.

7. Set up automatic saving.
   Automatic transfers between your checking and savings accounts are available almost everywhere. The timing, amount, and location of money transfers are all up to you. You can even split your direct deposit so that a portion of each paycheck goes into your savings account. The benefit is that you don't have to consider it and are less likely to spend the money on something else. Credit card incentives and spare change programs, which round up transactions to the nearest dollar and put the difference into a

savings or investing account, are additional simple savings strategies.

8. See your savings increase.
Every month, check your spending plan and assess your results. That will assist you in swiftly identifying and resolving issues and helping you stay to your personal savings goal. You could even be motivated to find more ways to save and achieve your goals quickly after learning to do so.

Chapter 2

Should You Purchase or Rent?

Outline of House Ownership vs. Renting

A significant component of the American Dream is property ownership. But deciding whether to buy or rent is a considerable choice that impacts your financial situation, way of life, and personal objectives. Depending on your lifestyle and financial position, you can select any one of the options. Both demand a consistent source of income (so you can afford the payments and related expenses) and may also involve some maintenance work.

Nonetheless, several distinctions clearly distinguish owning property from renting. Renting a house gives you more flexibility because you aren't always tethered to your home, and only some of the duties come with homeownership. Although owning a home gives you a sizable return on investment, it does so at a high cost, both now and in the long run.

Renting is more challenging than it sounds, and owning a home isn't always preferable. Here, we'll go through some main distinctions between renting and purchasing.

Housing Rental

The most pervasive misconception about renting is that you waste money every month. That is untrue. You must remember that having a place to reside always involves some financial outlay. Even while paying rent regularly doesn't help you develop equity, not all of the expenses associated with homeownership are related to doing so. Renting gives you complete control over your monthly housing expenses. Your lease specifies this sum so you can make appropriate plans. In rare situations, if you reside in a condominium, your landlord might also include homeowner association (HOA) dues, storage fees, and utility charges in that sum.

Every time your lease is up for renewal, you can experience rent hikes as a tenant. These rent increases may be even more pronounced if you live in particular areas of town. This might not be the case if you reside in a region where rent control and rent limits restrict how much a landlord can raise the rent.

If you rent, you can leave when your lease expires. But it also means that you can be forced to relocate quickly if your landlord decides to sell the land or convert your apartment building into condos. Less dramatically, they could raise the rent beyond your means.

Having a House Homeownership has both concrete and abstract advantages. You gain a sense of stability and pride in ownership in addition to having your own home and having control over its appearance and design.
But remember that since real estate is an illiquid asset, changing your mind about where you live can be very expensive. It could be difficult for you to sell when you desire. Even if you manage to, you might not be able to buy it for the price you wish, mainly if the property market is weak. High transaction costs are involved with selling your house, even if it's up.

Even if your mortgage payment is less than the rent, owning a property generally has higher overall costs than renting. Here are some expenses that, as a homeowner, you will incur that you would not typically incur as a renter:

Tax on real estate

- Pickup of trash (some landlords require renters to pay this)
- Services for sewer and water (some landlords need renters to pay this)
- Pest prevention
- Tree pruning
- Habitational insurance
- Pool maintenance (if you have one)
- Flood insurance required by the lender (in some areas)
- Earthquake protection (in some areas)

In the initial years of a long-term mortgage, mortgage interest may account for nearly all of your monthly payments. A 30-year mortgage may take up to 13 years before more of your income is applied to the principal. For a $100,000 loan with a 4% interest rate over 30 years, you'll pay around $72,000 in interest. You can recuperate part of that in tax deductions if you can itemize. Not to mention repairs and upkeep, which may be very expensive, you might discover that you have an unanticipated roof leak. Your roof replacement could cost an additional $12,000, which your home insurance policy might not cover.

Key variations
Real Estate Values
As was already said, homeownership is frequently promoted to increase wealth. The value of your property, however, can be impacted by several things, just like with any other investment, including:

- Economic problems
- Maintenance
- Environmental issues, such as adjacent hazardous waste dumps and landfills
- shabby interiors
- External factors (such as your obnoxious neighbor's front yard covered in pink flamingos) can also affect the value of your home.
- Houses in surplus
- Of course, as a tenant, you could also be impacted by these circumstances. Negative aspects, for instance, could assist in lowering your rent. After all, the landlord can need money and reduce the rent.

Tax Advantages

Some tax incentives may be available to homeowners. As long as deductions are itemized, the home mortgage interest deduction lowers any out-of-pocket costs incurred in the loan's early years.
Of course, you cannot deduct your mortgage interest from your taxes if you rent. Remember that you can still claim the standard deduction offered to all taxpayers. The same is true for homeowners who need more premises to itemize individually.

Maintenance and Repairs
As mentioned, being a homeowner entails responsibility for maintenance and routine upkeep. This can cost a lot of money. Furthermore, home improvement efforts rarely result in a value rise greater than their cost. According to Remodeling magazine, projects' prices exceed their values, with just around 60 cents of every dollar spent on repairs and improvements being recouped.

If you reside in a community with an HOA, it might relieve you of some homeownership responsibilities. Often, that will set you back a few hundred dollars every month. But be aware of the hassles that joining an association can bring. If you rent an apartment, your landlord will handle all repairs and maintenance. However, they might only be completed after some time or to your satisfaction.

You won't be enthusiastic about working on the spectacular initiatives yielding the most significant returns. The only project on Remodeling's list that comes close to recouping its total cost is replacing a garage door, which offers the best return.

Chapter 3

How to budget for a significant purchase

Thinking about the sum of money you'll need for a significant purchase, such as a wedding, a down payment on your first home, or a car loan, can be intimidating. Knowing how much you'll need to set aside monthly to achieve your goal is a beautiful place to start. Let's take the scenario where you want to have $10,000 saved up to help with part of the wedding costs, and you're getting married in 18 months. $555 per month is what

$10,000 divided by 18 months equals. That sounds like a lot of money because it is.

Finding strategies to save emergency money for a rainy day is always brilliant, even if you have yet to make a big purchase.
There is no quick way to save money. It necessitates patience, time, and effort. Yet, there are steps you may take to simplify the procedure.

1. Take care of yourself.
Pay yourself first, even if you cannot save enough money to reach your objective in the specified period. Set an automatic transfer from your checking account to your savings account on the day of your paycheck. By doing this, you can avoid the temptation to cut back on saving when a pay period concludes because you don't have enough money "left over." As it's considerably more challenging to cancel a direct deposit than to

cancel an Internet banking transfer, setting up a direct deposit with your company is even more foolproof.

2. Implement the 50/20/30 Rule
Financial success depends on effective money management and budgeting. The 50/20/30 Rule, which advises that you spend 50% of your take-home pay on necessities like food and rent or mortgage payments, 20% on savings and debt repayment, and 30% on lifestyle choices, has gained popularity thanks to Sen. Elizabeth Warren and LearnVest (workout equipment or the latest and greatest tech gadget). If your monthly take-home salary is $3,000 and you have no debt (congrats!), you should be setting aside $600 per month. You might save more money than you think!

3. Begin Small

Start small, even if it's just $50 or $100 per month, if 20 percent of your gross income seems like a lot. A little bit of saving is better than no saving at all, like working out, and you're much more likely to keep saving if you set small, attainable goals.

4. Put some cash into investments or a high-yield savings account.

Consider investing in a mutual fund, which often offers a better rate of return than regular savings or money market account, if you're saving money for something you won't buy for at least two or three years, such as a house. Consider transferring your interest earnings to a high-yield savings account to increase your interest earnings. However, you should know that the interest rate could change without prior notice.

To maintain your finances in good shape even during downturns, it's critical to assess market conditions and implement sensible tactics regularly.

And always remember that you should begin saving for retirement as soon as possible. Turbulent markets can present some of the best opportunities for long-term investors to build wealth so that early retirement account investments can position you for future success.

5. Start a Change Jar If Nothing Else

This is an excellent strategy to build up a little savings fund, even though it may seem overly straightforward, mainly if you utilize cash semi-regularly. Put the spare change in a jar and put it away whenever your wallet or pockets feel a little heavy or jangly. We've heard tales of folks using a 5-gallon water cooler container to save $3,000 or more.

There is no one-size-fits-all financial planning method, whether for saving for a wedding, a new house, or even to create and maintain excellent saving habits. But with these simple suggestions, you may position yourself for financial success and have faith in your choices.

Chapter 4

Why should you invest?

Investing is the best method to make your money work for you and accumulate wealth. Although keeping money in cash or bank savings accounts is considered a safe strategy, supporting it enables it to increase in value over time with the advantages of compounding and long-term growth. Investing aims to increase value and equity, create wealth, and generate future income. You can invest in stocks, bonds, mutual funds, options, futures, precious metals, real estate, or small businesses.

Why It's Vital to Invest at Any Age
Age, income, and risk profiles are just a few variables affecting a person's aspirations. The following three categories further categorize age:

- Young and beginning their careers
- Middle age and starting a family
- Age of retirement and independent

These demographics frequently fall short at the right time, with middle-aged people thinking about investments for the first time or older people obliged to budget and use the discipline they lacked as young individuals. You can't invest what you don't have; therefore, income is the prominent place to start when making investing plans. The first employment of a young adult serves as a wake-up call, requiring choices about IRA contributions, savings, or money market accounts, as well as the sacrifices necessary to balance growing affluence with the demand for immediate gratification. During this time, don't stress out over setbacks like being overwhelmed by your car and school loan payments or forgetting that your parents no longer pay the monthly credit card bill.

Outlook establishes the stage where we compete throughout our lives and the decisions that affect wealth management. For many people, family planning comes first on this list. Couples decide how many children they want, where they want to live, and how much money they need to make it happen. These calculations are frequently complicated by career expectations, with the highly educated enjoying enhanced earning power and others in low-level positions being obliged to make budget cuts.

There is always a right time to start investing. Before you realize that life is going swiftly and that you must make arrangements for retirement and old age, you can be well into middle age. When setting investment goals too late, fear may take over, but fear should vanish once the strategy is in motion. Regardless of your age, income, or mindset, always remember that all investments begin with the first dollar. But, people who invest for a long time have an edge since their wealth grows, enabling them to live a lifestyle that others cannot.

The top 7 reasons to invest your money are as follows:

1. Develop your finances.
Increase the value of your money by investing it. Most investment options, including stocks, certificates of deposit, and

bonds, provide long-term returns on your capital. Thanks to this return, your money can grow and become more valuable.

2. Invest in retirement

It would help if you started saving money for retirement while working. Invest your retirement funds in diverse assets, including equities, bonds, mutual funds, real estate, companies, and precious metals. As you reach retirement age, you can continue living off these investments' income.

Consider taking on more risk with your assets when you're younger, depending on your risk tolerance. Your odds of becoming richer grow as your level of risk rises. As you begin to get older and closer to retirement, you should invest more conservatively.

3. Generate greater returns

Your money needs to be invested in a place where it can earn a higher rate of return if you want it to expand. You will make more money if the rate of return is higher. Compared to savings accounts, investment vehicles often provide the chance to earn higher rates of return. So, consider investing your money if you want the opportunity to get a better return.

4. Meet financial objectives

You can achieve significant financial goals by investing. You will make more money over the long run and more quickly if your investments yield a better rate of return than a savings account. You can utilize this investment return to help you achieve critical financial objectives like buying a home, or a car, starting your own business, or paying for your children's college.

5. Increase pre-tax income

You can invest your pre-tax money in some investment vehicles, such as employer-sponsored 401(k)s. By choosing this option, you can save more money than if you were limited to investing after-tax money.

6. Be eligible for employer-matching initiatives

Some employers will match the funds you put into your 401(k) plan up to a certain amount. Of course, investing regularly in your 401(k) plan is the only way you may be eligible for and receive this matching money. So many people contribute to their 401(k)s to receive matching employer contributions.

7. Establish and grow a business

The development and growth of a firm depend heavily on investment. Many investors enjoy assisting businesses and helping to produce new goods and jobs. They take pleasure in starting up new enterprises, growing them into successful organizations, and reaping the financial benefits.

Chapter 5

Investments you should make.

Investors with sound judgment avoid putting all of their eggs in one basket. Instead, individuals become familiar with a few distinct investment kinds and employ their understanding of each to profit in various ways.

There are several options available when it comes to investing. But before investing your money and putting together your portfolio, you must know all your alternatives.

Every investment strategy has advantages and disadvantages. The ideal investments depend on your risk tolerance, market knowledge, the window of time to prevent capital gains, and initial investment goals. Indeed, a few investments among the wide varieties available will be successful for you, so let's get started.

1. Commodities and money
   While cash and commodities are often seen as low-risk investment categories, starting with one of these choices may be a brilliant idea if you're new to investing or are uneasy with any risk. Remember that investments with low risk typically have low returns.

- **Gold**

  You can invest in commodities
  like gold, silver, and crude oil.
  Although gold has a long history,
  it is sometimes a wise choice.
  Since gold is a commodity, its
  price is determined by scarcity
  and fear, which can cause
  government decisions or
  environmental alterations that
  can influence your investment in
  gold, be aware that the price can
  fluctuate wildly and quickly
  because your "moat" (protection
  against a price reduction) is
  depending on outside sources.
  When there is a lot of shortage
  and fear, the price tends to rise;
  when gold is abundantly
  available, the price tends to fall.

If you believe that the world will become a terrifying place in the future, then gold could be a good investment for you.

- **Bank items and CDs**
  Savings accounts and money market accounts are examples of the investment prodUnlikebanks offer. Like savings accounts, the money market often provides more excellent interest rates in exchange for higher minimum balance requirements.
  Another banking product is a CD or certificate of deposit. When you buy a CD, you consent to lend the bank a certain amount of money for a specific period in exchange for a greater interest rate than you would receive from a standard savings account.

CDs are incredibly low-risk investments, yet low-risk investments typically have modest returns. A return on CDs often offered by banks is less than 2% annually, which is insufficient to keep up with inflation.

- **Cryptocurrency**
  One of the more recent investing categories is cryptocurrency. These are uncontrolled digital currencies that may be bought and exchanged on exchanges. Due to their rapid and dramatic growth, cryptocurrencies like Bitcoin and Dogecoin have attracted much attention as investment vehicles in recent

years. Nonetheless, they continue to be hazardous investments due to their numerous unknowable aspects of them.

Government regulation is a possibility, and there's also a chance that people will only accept cryptocurrencies as a means of payment. Since cryptocurrency currently has no intrinsic value, it might vanish as quickly as it appeared.

Methods for Buying Bitcoin

You can swap your US dollars for cryptocurrencies like you can trade them for any other money, such as Yen or Euros.

Despite not technically being a part of the Forex market, investment in cryptocurrency works very similarly. The value of cryptocurrencies, which are very easy to purchase online, is something that many cryptocurrency buyers anticipate would increase versus the dollar.

If someone bought Bitcoin in 2013 and sold it today, they would undoubtedly make excellent profits. The issue is that timing the cryptocurrency market is impossible. Bitcoin and other cryptocurrencies may experience steep price rises or declines to zero.

2. Bonds and Investments
    Other low-risk investment options include bonds and securities. The US government, state and local governments, and private businesses sell bonds.
    A type of bond known as mortgage-backed securities can be issued by

either a private company or a government agency in the United States.

Investment funds comprise a pool of money gathered from numerous people and invested in various securities, including stocks, bonds, and other assets. The group of investments often follows an index of the market.

A mutual fund

A mutual fund is a particular form of investment fund run by a money manager who invests your money on your behalf and makes an effort to maximize returns.

Mutual funds often combine stocks and bonds, but they carry less risk because your money is spread across various equities and bonds. Only stock dividends, bond interest, or sales made when the fund's value rises along with the market will provide you gains. Regarding value, keep in mind that mutual funds are created and managed by alleged "financial experts" who struggle to outperform the market, particularly when you consider the fees they are asking you to manage your money in the first place.

Index Funds

One stock investment option that diversifies your investment over several stocks is index funds, which are similar to mutual funds. Unlike mutual funds, a money manager does not directly manage index funds; instead, they are passively managed.

There are fewer fees associated with index funds because they are passively managed, which increases the possibility of slightly better returns than mutual funds. Your returns, however, will depend on how well the index your fund tracks performs. Given that the most significant indices are used to monitor the market's general movement, their long-term performance is comparable to the market's. In other words, they typically produce an annual average return of around 7%.

3. The Stock Exchange
   The stock market can be entered into in a variety of ways. As I just indicated, you can invest in a stock market index, stock options, or—and this is my personal favorite—individual stocks.

Individual Stocks

Stocks represent "shares" of ownership in a specific business. You take a partial ownership interest in a firm when you buy its shares. This implies that when the firm is profitable, you are as well, and when the company's value increases, so does the value of your stock.

The value of an owner's investment in a company increases when its share price increases. The owner can then make a profit by selling the stock. However, the value of the owner's investment decreases when the price of a company's stock rises.

If a corporation decides to pay dividends to its shareholders, stockholders can also benefit from these payments.

Investing in carefully chosen, individually researched businesses can generate significantly more than average returns. By only investing in fantastic firms at prices that provide a significant return, you can reduce your risk.

4. Planning for retirement
The two main categories of retirement funds are the 401K and the IRA. The money you save and invest in various ways makes up both accounts. Retirement account risk and return are entirely based on the investments made, which can be made in a wide range of securities. Another investment kind that you could consider as part of your retirement plan, outside these retirement accounts, is an annuity.

401k

A 401(k) is the name of an employer-sponsored retirement account (k). The primary benefit of selecting this retirement plan is the potential for a "match" from your employer, which means they will make a matching contribution to your account up to a certain proportion.

5. Buying homes, apartments, and commercial buildings, house flipping, owning farms and trailer parks, and other real estate investing methods are all possible. For most new investors, the biggest drawback is the entry fee.

6. Property

As an expensive investment, real estate can quickly push away smaller investors with less money.

For those who wish to engage in real estate but need more money, crowd-funded investment alternatives are starting to materialize.

The most challenging aspect of real estate investing is locating a home you can buy with a margin of safety. If you can pull that off, investment in real estate can yield respectable returns.

In addition to renting or leasing the property to tenants, you can profit by purchasing the asset at a discount and reselling it for market value.

Just continue buying

.

Chapter 6

What time frame should I invest in?

When to begin investing: 4 indications that you're ready
How can you tell when you're prepared to start investing? Perhaps you are and didn't even realize it. Here are some benchmarks to aid your decision.

Nowadays, there is a lot of talk about investment. Should you include it in your plan? How can you tell when you're prepared to begin investing? Perhaps you are and didn't even realize it.

According to an old proverb, it's more important to invest over time than to time the market, says Heather Winston, Principal Assistant Director of financial advising and planning. And beginning to invest as early as possible, even with ostensibly small sums of money, may set you up for future success.

These are four cues that could aid in your decision-making.

1. You're putting money aside for emergencies.
Life can be unpredictable. To provide yourself with the stability that investing may require, creating an emergency fund with at least three months' worth of costs is a good

idea. You won't need to draw on investments set aside for longer-term objectives because your emergency fund will act as a safety net in the event of an unforeseen event. After your emergency fund is off to a strong start, you can balance investing and saving by allocating funds to both.

2. You have extra cash at the end of each month.
Your emergency savings are doing well. All of the invoices and high-interest obligations are paid in full. You have enough money on hand to pay your bills. Are there any leftovers? It is not necessary to have much. Starting small and building those funds over time is the key to investing (more on that below). The secret is to persevere so that your investment can pay off.

3. You're prepared to commit to some monetary objectives.

Knowing your destination will make investing a more successful journey. Goals can help you with that by giving you focus and direction.

Start by saving for short-term objectives like a big vacation, a wedding, or even a down payment on a home, advises Winston. Long-term requirements, like retirement savings, may seem more manageable if you've shown yourself that you can accomplish a shorter-term goal.

4. A retirement plan is accessible to you. A 401(k) (k). A 403(b) (b). If you can contribute to one of these employer-sponsored retirement plans, you may have made significant progress toward investing. You can have money deducted from each paycheck to invest in most employer-sponsored retirement plans. Because of this, saving money for retirement is much simpler.

Even better, some firms promise to match workers' payments to a set amount. That is free money, and those additional donations can be very beneficial in the long run.

Do you have an extra $100 a month to invest? Even modest sums over time might build up.

Your investments could increase in value. For 30 years, you could put $100 a month in a jar and collect $36,000. Thanks to compound interest, the same money invested at a 6% annual rate of return would rise to about $100,000 in the same length of time.

Consider investing through a 401(k), IRA, or another type of retirement account. There are also a lot of opportunities there. A 1% increase in pre-tax contributions would only subtract roughly $10 from your biweekly take-home pay if you earned $35,000 annually.

That could result in an additional $150 monthly to spend later in retirement.

Chapter 7

The Most Valuable Asset

Which assets are valuable or will otherwise increase your net worth? Here is a list of 10 essential assets.

1. Possessing a primary residence Homeownership is one of the most popular ways to enhance their net worth significantly. Choose a 15- or 20-year term instead of the standard 30-year mortgage so you may pay it off faster, creating a sizable asset and saving money on interest. Also, as long as you are married and filing jointly, capital gains are

tax-free, up to $500,000 if you decide to sell your property after paying it off.

In some expensive urban regions, renting may make more financial sense than buying, depending on whether the cost of ownership is affordable compared to overall living costs.

Second Residence

Second houses are an intelligent approach to generating passive income using websites for short-term rentals like Homeaway, VRBO, or Airbnb. You can first utilize the additional revenue to contribute to a quicker mortgage payoff. Once the mortgage is paid off, you'll own a sizable asset and continue receiving passive income from renting it out if you choose. Both of these outcomes can lead to a nice increase in your net worth.

3. Investing in Retirement

Even though retirement may be decades away, saving money now will increase your net worth.

You can begin saving for retirement right away, and tax-deferred accounts, like a 401(k) or a regular IRA, can accelerate the growth of your savings account balance. Make it a point to maximize your retirement contributions by setting aside a specific sum each pay period, especially if your employer matches your payments. You will continuously save money if you approach it as a budget item, enabling it to develop and raise your net worth.

4. Education

Your education credentials would be among your most valuable assets, even if you hadn't previously considered them in this way. You may invest in your education to improve your chances of getting a better job or promotion.

Over time, this decision could pay off financially. Therefore, after earning your bachelor's degree, your education continues. You may obtain a student loan from a credit union if it offers parent loan alternatives through Sallie Mae Bank or a lending partner, in addition to in-school student loan options, to assist with the cost of continuing education classes or certifications.

If you're still not persuaded, take into account this: A promotion or annual raise that you obtain as a result of further schooling can come considerably more quickly than the $6,000 in additional income that would otherwise need you to save $300,000 in a savings account yielding 2% interest.

5. Rental Property
You successfully increase your net worth when you buy rental properties with bank money. When you start renting out the

homes, utilize the income to settle the mortgages rather than taking money out of your savings. Your real estate will increase in equity, and its market worth should rise over time.

If you have real estate knowledge but have yet to be ready to buy properties on your own, you can find investors to help with the down payment if you receive a share of the ownership. Also, once you've secured financing for the rental property, you can agree on a management fee with the investors.

6. Health

The key to increasing your net worth is maintaining excellent health. You can work longer hours and be more productive without spending a fortune on doctor visits, procedures, or treatments. You can invest in your health by eating correctly, getting regular exercise, and seeing your doctor for checkups.

7. Saving for college

When it comes time to use the funds for the school, many parents assume ownership of a 529 college savings plan for their kids, which boosts their net worth. So far, the funds are used for eligible educational costs, withdrawals from 529 plans remain tax-free, and the funds grow tax-free.

Also, the cash may be moved between beneficiaries without incurring fees or taxes. For instance, money could be allocated among several siblings.

8. Keep Your House in Good Condition

Investing in preserving your home makes sense as it is one of your most significant possessions. Increase your return on investment when it's time to sell by repairing your roof, maintaining your gutters, and periodically servicing your HVAC system. On the other hand, neglecting your house can present opportunities for prospective buyers to use a lack of upkeep to negotiate a lower price, leaving you with less money.

9. Household products
Consider the larger picture, even if you don't think buying a new laptop or refrigerator will increase your net worth.

Like purchasing a vehicle, it pays to buy the highest-quality, most durable stuff you can manage but also consider how quickly these items lose value. Investing in high-quality things increases your net worth because it leaves more money in the bank than continually paying repair costs and replacing appliances, which can be expensive. Get the best discounts, compare items, and read reviews to decide which brands and models are the best investments.

10. Personal Loans

You can increase your net worth by earning passive income by acting as someone else's bank. Investments that involve lending money to private individuals or organizations in exchange for interest include personal loans, notes, and trust deeds.

With these kinds of investments, you'll continue to earn a fixed rate of return whether the underlying asset's value rises or falls, giving you the money you can reinvest to increase your wealth.

Consider consulting a professional with considerable experience for assistance, such as a broker, entity, or regulated and adequately licensed partner, to ensure you comprehend the ins and outs of a potential investment to protect your interests.

Conclusion

Find areas where you can cut back if your expenses exceed your income.

This could be as simple as packing your lunch or canceling your gym membership. Keep a spending journal and record every purchase you make in a month.

Alternatively, if you use your credit or debit card for most purchases, examine the statement from the previous month to determine where your money is going.

Encourage everyone in your household to participate in sticking to a budget.

Make a plan that you can all follow together while sitting down.

Calculate the available spending money and decide how much you will receive.

Even though schemes to become rich quickly occasionally may seem alluring, the tried-and-true method of accumulating wealth is via consistent saving and investing—and patiently waiting for that money to grow over time. Starting little is acceptable. Starting early and consistently is crucial. Make money, save it, and then wisely invest it. Insurance can help you safeguard your assets while reducing your tax liability.

Understand that accumulating wealth is a process rather than a final goal. Throughout the road, celebrate your accomplishments and resist the urge to give up because of setbacks or difficulties. You can succeed financially and accumulate wealth over time if you have patience, discipline, and a clear understanding of your objectives.